SPIDERS

SPIDERS

CHARTWELL
BOOKS, INC.

Published by Chartwell Books
A Division of Book Sales Inc.
114 Northfield Avenue
Edison, New Jersey 08837
USA

ISBN 0-7858-0980-5

This book is produced by
Quantum Books Ltd
6 Blundell Street
London N7 9BH

Project Manager: Rebecca Kingsley
Project Editor: Judith Millidge
Design/Editorial: David Manson
Andy McColm, Maggie Manson

The material in this publication previously appeared in
The Book of Spiders, Exotic Pet Survival Guide

QUMAFS
Set in Futura
Reproduced in Singapore by Eray Scan
Printed in Singapore by Star Standard Industries (Pte) Ltd

Contents

SPECTACULAR SPIDERS

Many people can be unfairly
squeamish to our subjects for
although a number of spiders are
harmful to humans, they do not
seek to be so. The majority are
totally harmless, and in fact are
great allies in the destruction of
many more harmful insect pests.
Some are spectacularly colored,
such as this orb weaver (left),
while others, like the jumping
spiders, are quite charming
little creatures.

Evolution and Biology

To the uninitiated, the arachnida are probably thought of as similar to insects, but with four pairs of legs. However, because they are carnivorous and, have an ability to produce silk, they are distinctly different to other insects.

CARNIVOROUS SPIDERS

Since arachnids are carnivorous, they all show well-developed adaptations and strong jaws for capturing and killing their prey. Spiders and scorpions also have a means to paralyse the prey with poison. Silk is produced by other insects, but only spider's silk has so many variations, each with its own special function.

ORIGINS OF ARACHNIDA

There is still some doubt as to the precise origins of spiders. They certainly originated in the sea, and it is believed that their common ancestor was not unlike a king crab in appearance. The most recent research indicates that the arachnida have evolved into two groups : those with and those without extensor leg muscles.

Left. The Lobed Argiope (A.Lobata) spins the web of a mature spider.

Above. The African Golden Orb Weaver is widespread in subtropical regions.

INSECT DISTINCTIONS

Apart from the difference in the number of legs, spiders differ from other insects in the way the body is divided. In other insects, the body is divided into head, thorax and abdomen whereas in the arachnids head and thorax are fused together in some groups to form the prosoma and in others all three divisions are fused into a single structure. Another clear distinction is that insects always have a pair of antennae.

FOSSIL RECORD

The fossil record of spiders is not very good, as they are relatively soft-bodied creatures and therefore do not easily fossilize. A recent find of a nearly complete spider spinneret from the Middle Devonian period shows that some spiders were quite advanced around 380 million years ago. No fossils of flying insects have been found from as early so this spider must have been a predator of ground-dwelling insects.

Living Spiders

The families of living spiders have representatives in all regions of the world; in fact anywhere that segmented insects or arthropods are found, spiders are likely to be found nearby preying on them.

SURROUNDED BY SPIDERS

Some spiders live on the seashore, where they are submerged under the ocean twice a day. Fresh water is, of course, the habitat of the well-known water spider, *Argyroneta aquatica*, and other species are able to submerge themselves. Many spiders live in underground cave systems and the only places lacking spiders are the north and south poles.

SPIDER SIZES

They vary in size from the giant theraphosid bird-eating spiders whose legs would span a dinner-plate, down to symphytognathids which could sit on, and just about span the eye of one of the aforementioned giants. The largest spiders have a body up to 3in long with a span across the legs of some 10in. Females tend to be larger.

Left. The Fishing Spider spends most of its time on or near ponds.

Above. The Flower Spider has the ability to change color from white to yellow.

SPIDER SUB-ORDERS

Spiders are divided into three sub-orders: the primitive and rare Liphistiomorphae, the Mygalo-morphae and the Araneomorphae. The Liphistiomorphae are seldom seen, being burrowing spiders from tropical Asia. The spiders in this book come from the other groups:
1. The Mygalomorphae including tarantulas, trapdoor spiders and purse web spiders.
2. The Araneomorphae, usually called true spiders, comprising the remaining types.

SPIDER JAW MECHANISMS

The primitive Liphistiidae and the mygalomorph spiders have their jaws arranged so that they strike down against the prey walking on the ground or another hard surface. Araneomorph spiders' jaws work independent from any surface, since they move toward each other when in action. The prey becomes impaled between them. The latter system is much more efficient since it allows a spider to catch prey on the flimsy structure of its web.

Spider Sense Organs

The only sense organs easily visible with the aid of a magnifying glass are the spider's eyes. Unlike the compound eyes of the insects, spiders have simple eyes and the majority have extremely poor eyesight depending on their other senses to capture their prey.

THE EYES

The eyes are of two types. Main eyes, always the center pair of the front row, possess a lens and a retina. These eyes are well developed in spiders that are active hunters; otherwise they are small and are absent in the six-eyed spiders. The rest of the eyes are secondary, with light-sensitive cells in the retina that point away from light rather than toward it.

TASTE AND SMELL

Whether the senses of taste and smell are separate in spiders is debatable. We know that spiders can taste with the oesophagus, for unpalatable food is rejected fast, but they also possess a sense of taste-by-touch sited on the tips of the palps and legs. Tiny openings on the legs, referred to as tarsal organs, are also associated with taste and/or smell.

Left. The Pan Tropical Jumper is an alert mobile hunter with good eyesight.

Above. The Zebra Spider clearly showing the sensory hairs covering the body.

SENSORY RECEPTORS

Spiders do not hear like we do, but they have a well-developed ability to sense vibrations, both airborne and those transmitted through the surface on which they are standing. This sensory ability is sited in quite a number of different receptors spread around their body, but especially on the appendages. Structures called trichobothria are found on certain leg segments and consist of an upright hair set in a socket. Trichobothria respond to vibrations from moving insects; the way they move allows the spider to decide the direction the insect is coming from. Sensory hairs are found all over the body of the spider and only a single one needs to be touched to elicit an immediate response. Spiders also have many temperature receptors on their body surface. Being cold-blooded, they must maintain their body heat within certain necessary limits by means of behavioral patterns.

13

Communication and Silk

It may come as a surprise to learn that a number of spider families communicate with each other by sound. Spiders have no ears, but their many body vibration receptors 'hear' the vibrations in the air.

ACOUSTIC COMMUNCIATION

Sound is most commonly made by scraping one or more spines over a set of ridges. Sound production like this, as in grasshoppers, is called stridulation. Sound is used in courtship, male aggression and in defense. The advantage of making the correct sound is clear since any intruder into a spider's territory is potential prey. Failure to indicate friendly intent, could well end up in cannabilism.

CHEMICAL COMMUNICATION

The other form of communication is that of sex scents or pheromones. Pheromones are volatile chemicals secreted by spiders, which enable them to determine the sex of any spider they meet or whose silk they come into contact with. Spider silk is coated in these chemicals. The male spider, for example, is then able to find a female of his own species by following her dragline or coming across her web.

Left. The Wolf Weaver spider carries her egg sac attached to her spinnerets leaving her jaws free to catch prey.

Above. A female Mouse Spider, commonly found in European houses, protecting her egg sac with silk.

SILK PRODUCTION

For most spiders, silk plays a major part in their everyday life. It is believed it evolved originally as a means of lining the burrow, and then of protecting the eggs either from drying out or from predators. Only later did it also come to be used in the capture and wrapping of prey. Silk is produced by the abdominal silk glands and at least seven different kinds are known to exist. Each gland produces its own kind of silk for a specific function.

No spider family possesses all seven types and the cylindrical gland which exudes female silk for wrapping egg sacs is absent in males. Silk is produced as a liquid and is emitted from the spinnerets much like squeezing toothpaste from a tube. The liquid silk sets as the spider pulls on it. The harder the spider pulls the stronger the silk. As it oozes out and sets, the silk is manipulated by the spider into the marvelous webs typical of their species.

SPIDER SPECIES

Key to symbols
A number of icons are used to provide a snapshot of each spider. These are explained below.

Size of body (in)

<u>Habitat</u>

 Grassy areas scrub and heath   Semi-aquatic

 Woodland areas   Aquatic

 Tropical forests   Mountains and caves

 Desert and arid areas   Buildings

<u>Diet</u>

 Insectivorous   Carnivorous

Fish   Vegetation

<u>Danger!</u>

Venomous species

Treat these spiders with extreme caution

PURSE-WEB SPIDER

The web of this species looks like the finger of a glove. Insects that land on the web are bitten through the webbing. Once the spider has eaten, the remains are discarded, and the web repaired. The jaws are large and the legs short.

Scientific name *Atypus affinis*.
Female Size $2/3$in.
Male Size $3/8$in.
Habitat Grassland and shrubby places, in sandy or chalky areas.
Range Europe, N Africa, W Asia.

2/3in

AUSTRALIAN TRAP DOOR SPIDER

The female has a low, reddish-brown carapace with eyes on a tubercle and a pale brown abdomen. The male is similar but thinner. In the mating season, the male uses the spurs on his front legs to keep the female jaws out of the way.

Scientific name *Aname sp.*
Female Size $1^1/4$in.
Male Size $7/8$in.
Habitat Soil suitable for burrowing in open areas.
Range Western Australia.

1^1/4in

PINK-TOED TARANTULA

This is a well-known spider because of its orange and pink 'toes'. Their abdomen and carapace are covered in long hairs. They construct a silky nest in banana leaves and occasionally catch roosting birds, but mostly they eat tree frogs and other insects.

Scientific name *Avicularia avicularia*.
Female Size 2in.
Male Size 1¹/3in.
Habitat Trees and hollow stumps in humid forests.
Range Guyana, Brazil, Venezuela, Trinidad.

GOLIATH TARANTULA

This is the largest spider in the world. It is capable of eating frogs, toads, mice, lizards and occasionally small snakes. Their legs are covered in hairs. They are able to make clear sounds by rubbing parts of their bodies together.

Scientific name *Theraphosa blondi*.
Female Size 3¹/2in.
Male Size 3³/8in.
Habitat Tropical rainforests in deep burrows.
Range Venezuela, N Brazil, Guyana, Suriname.

MEXICAN RED-KNEE TARANTULA

This large tarantula is easily identified by the orange or red knees. The abdomen can be brown or black and the carapace is black with orange at the edges. They have become popular pets due to their attractive coloring, and can need protection, in the wild, because of this popularity. They eat beetles, lizards and millipedes and can live for several years.

Scientific name *Brachypelma smithi.*
Female Size 3in.
Male Size 2^1/4in.
Habitat Scrubland, stony areas and shady forest banks.
Range Mexico.

3in

INDIAN BLACK AND WHITE TARANTULA

This spider has very attractive pattern-ing, more so than the zebra spider. They have yellow markings on the first two pairs of legs. The abdomen has a central cream band edged in black. The carapace is gray with cream markings. This is a popular tarantula and the cost of buying adult stock can be high. These spiders are nocturnal and live in trees where their nest is usually built in a tree hole.

Scientific name *Poecilotheria regalis.*
Female Size 2^1/2in.
Male Size 2in.
Habitat Tropical rainforest and buildings.
Range Asia.

2^1/2in

MEXICAN BLOND TARANTULA

A brown spider which burrows in dry, arid country. The carapace is beige and contrasts with the darker abdomen. They are nocturnal, hunting ants and small vertebrates. During the day, they keep in their burrows and cover the entrance with silk threads.

Scientific name *Aphonopelma chalcodes.*
Female Size 2³/₈in.
Male Size 1³/₄in.
Habitat Arid, dry places with low humidity.
Range Arizona, Mexico.

2³/₈in

CHILEAN ROSE TARANTULA

This species is sometimes known as the Chilean Red-Back is not to be confused with the deadly Australian Red-Back, a close relative. This is a burrowing species, which likes high humidity. They will eat many types of small invertebrates. This tarantula is pale brown and pink in color.

Scientific name *Grammostola cala.*
Female Size 1¹/₂in.
Male Size 1¹/₃in.
Habitat Arid, dry places with low humidity.
Range Arizona, Mexico.

1¹/₂in

ZEBRA TARANTULA

Despite its name, this tarantula is black. The creamy-white stripes on the legs give it the Zebra name. These are the best known tarantulas, which burrow and can move very quickly. Their burrows can extend to a depth of 5in, the entrance being carefully concealed with leaves.

Scientific name *Aphonopelma seemanni*.
Female Size 2³/8in.
Male Size 1³/4in.
Habitat Arid, dry places.
Range Costa Rica.

2³/8in

VELVET TARANTULA

Another burrowing tarantula which hunts by night on the floor of the rainforest. The carapace and abdomen are dark brown, the legs are paler brown with blue streaks. The back two pairs of legs are much hairier than the front legs.

Scientific name *Lyrognathus robustus*.
Female Size 2in.
Male Size 1¹/3in.
Habitat Tropical rainforests.
Range Malaysia.

2in

COMMON BABOON SPIDER

This species is recognized by a deep transverse groove in the center of the carapace. In the female, the carapace is dark-gray, and the abdomen is a ginger color. The male carapace is dark with reddish hairs on his abdomen. They dig holes but are known to use empty animal burrows.

Scientific name *Harpactira sp.*
Female Size 2in.
Male Size 1^{1}/2in.
Habitat Grassland and scrubby areas.
Range South Africa.

ANDEAN SPITTING SPIDER

The venom glands of this spider are housed in the domed carapace and produce a poisonous gum. They have long legs and are mainly beige in color.

Scientific name *Scytodes globula.*
Female Size 3^1/2in.
Male Size 2^3/4in.
Habitat Caves, buildings, under stones.
Range Argentina, Chile.

NET THROWING SPIDER

This spider looks like a twig during the day. At night it hangs upside down and holds a net in its front legs. The spider is very quick to place the postage stamp sized net where it will catch insects who try to crawl or fly past. They are also known as the Ogre-faced Spider.

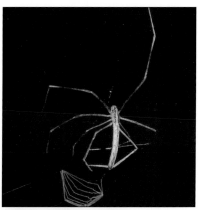

Scientific name *Deinopis longipes.*
Female Size 2/3in.
Male Size 1/3in.
Habitat Tropical rainforests, walls and gardens.
Range Central America.

BLACK WIDOW

The female spider is easily recognized by the red 'hourglass' marking on the underside. They are highly venomous. The male is much smaller and does not bite. The female is able to overcome larger creatures by throwing a sticky gummy silk at them as they struggle in the web.

Scientific name *Larrodectus mactans*.
Female Size 2/3in.
Male Size 1/5in.
Habitat Plantations, stony areas and buildings.
Range Southern USA.

GRASS FUNNEL-WEAVER

This spider has a chevron pattern on its abdomen and a brown carapace with three pale bands. The prey landing on the sheet-web brings out the spider, which dashes out to drag the prey back.

Scientific name *Agelena labyrinthica.*
Female Size 1/2in.
Male Size 1/3in.
Habitat Shrubby and grassy places.
Range Europe, Asia and Japan.

1/2in

LONG-JAWED ORB-WEAVER

A long-legged spider with a striped abdomen and brown carapace. Often seen stretched out at the center of its web. Their diet depends on where the web is built. If constructed near water, they eat aquatic insects.

Scientific name *Tetragnatha montana.*
Female Size 3/8in.
Male Size 1/3in.
Habitat Damp woods, marshes, ponds and streams.
Range Europe, N Africa, Asia, Japan, N America.

3/8in

AFRICAN GOLDEN ORB-WEAVER

This spider hangs head-down on its web. The female has a dark, elongated abdomen and is marked with a white, oblong ring and white bars. The carapace has silvery hairs and the legs have black and yellow bands. The male can sometimes be found in the female's web.

Scientific name *Nephila senegalensis.*
Female Size 1 1/3in.
Male Size 1/4in.
Habitat Forests edges and tracks.
Range Gambia to S Africa.

1 1/3in

GOLDEN ORB-WEAVER

These spiders build large webs and the female sits at the web's hub, which is made of high-strength silk. The female has a carapace which is gray and brown and her abdomen is dark olive-brown with pale spots. The male is brown with darker legs.

Scientific name *Nephila clavipes*.
Female Size $1^1/3$in.
Male Size $^1/3$in.
Habitat Forest, swamps and shady spots.
Range Caribbean, S America, Central and SE USA.

$1^1/3$in

MADAGASCAN ORB-WEAVER

A large golden orb-weaving spider with an almost conical abdomen. The front of the abdomen is white with a wedge-shaped marking of yellow and gray. The carapace and legs are black with a tinge of red. The male is small and brown.

Scientific name *Nephila inaurata*.
Female Size 1^1/3in.
Male Size ^{1}/6in.
Habitat Forests edges and tracks, gardens.
Range Africa, Madagascar, Seychelles.

1^1/3in

COMMON GARDEN SPIDER

One of the most common spiders in the northern hemisphere. The female's abdomen has a pale cross of white or yellow spots on it. The abdomen itself, can be brown, beige, black or red. The eyes are in two rows. The male is smaller, brown,and has a white pattern on its abdomen.

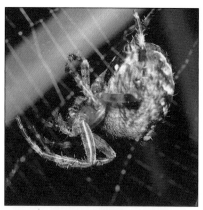

Scientific name *Araneus diadematus*.
Female Size ^{5}/8in.
Male Size ^{1}/3in.
Habitat Woodlands, gardens, road-sides and scrub.
Range Europe, N America, Asia, Japan.

^{5}/8in

FOUR SPOT ORB-WEAVER

The female has a large, abdomen which can be either yellow, green, red or brown and marked with four large and other smaller, white spots. The male is banded on the body and legs and the abdomen is brown with white marks. They feed on grasshoppers and other insects.

Scientific name *Araneus quadratus.*
Female Size $2/3$in.
Male Size $1/3$in.
Habitat Scrub, heathland, grassland.
Range Europe, Asia.

SILVER ARGIOPE

The female has a silvery carapace. The back of the abdomen has five lobes and is silver and orange or yellow. The web is built near the ground where the spider catches mostly jumping insects. The male is smaller and pale brown with two dark bands along the abdomen.

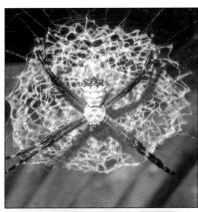

Scientific name *Argiope argentata.*
Female Size $5/8$in.
Male Size $1/6$in.
Habitat Scrubland, gardens, woods.
Range Southern USA, Argentina.

BRUENNICHI'S ARGIOPE

This spider can also be known as the Wasp Spider because of the black and yellow and white banding on the female's abdomen. The carapace is silvery and the legs are banded dark and pale. The web is low-built to catch jumping insects such as grasshoppers. The male tries to mate with the female as soon as her old skin is shed, this can sometimes be fatal for the male.

Scientific name *Argiope bruennichi.*
Female Size $^7/8$in.
Male Size $^1/4$in.
Habitat Woodland edges, road-sides, grassy areas.
Range Europe, Asia, China, Japan.

$^7/8$in

LOBED ARGIOPE

This is a common spider of the Mediterranean region. The abdomen of the female is silvery or beige and has six to nine lobes. The vertical webs are built in the summer to catch large, flying insects. The male is smaller and slim bodied.

Scientific name *Argiope lobata.*
Female Size $^7/_8$in.
Male Size $^1/_4$in.
Habitat Dry, hot scrubland, roadside verges and edges of woods.
Range Europe, Asia.

$^7/_8$in

MULTI-COLORED ARGIOPE

This is a very colorful spider with yellow, brown and white banding, a pentagonal abdomen and a silvery carapace. The female appears to have just four legs as she sits on the vertical web, but she extends her legs out along the four zigzag bands which form a cross – the stabilimentum.

Scientific name *Argiope versicolor.*
Female Size $3/8$in.
Male Size $1/6$in.
Habitat Tropical forest edges and clearings.
Range Asia.

GREEN ORB WEAVER

A spider which is common in many areas but not often seen, as it blends so well among the leaves with its green color. The carapace of both sexes is brown while the abdomen is bright green with some yellow and red markings underneath. The web is often distorted in shape, is small and usually hidden among leaves.

Scientific name *Araniella cucurbitina.*
Female Size $1/4$in.
Male Size $1/6$in.
Habitat Woodland areas and gardens.
Range Europe, Asia, Japan, Africa.

$1/4$in

ORIENTAL DOME-WEAVER

This spider constructs a complicated web, which can sometimes join up to other webs close by. They will hang upside down below the center. The female carapace is pale gray, with pale brown legs which can have bands of red or brown. The abdomen can be either white or yellow, patterned with black markings. There are two dark-tipped humps near the front of the abdomen. The male is small and pale brown in color.

Scientific name *Cyrtophora moluccensis.*
Female Size 2/3in.
Male Size 1/6in.
Habitat Forest edges, against pylons and fences.
Range India, Asia.

2/3in

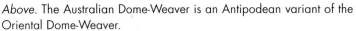
Above. The Australian Dome-Weaver is an Antipodean variant of the Oriental Dome-Weaver.

BARK SPIDER

This spider has a strange appearance with leathery protuberances on the abdomen which act as camouflage against the tree bark. The eyes are located on a bump at the front of the carapace. This is a nocturnal species which constructs its web during the night and dismantles it in the early dawn. During the day they remain still, resting on branches.

Scientific name *Caerostris sexcuspidata.*
Female Size 2/3in.
Male Size 1/6in.
Habitat Thorn trees.
Range Africa, Asia.

2/3in

SCORPION ORB-WEAVER

This spider has an elongated abdomen with two horns at the front and a star-shaped tip at the end. When the spider closes its legs, it resembles a dry twig. If the spider is frightened, the end of the abdomen curls up like a scorpion's tail. The usual position of this spider is upside down, looking like a rolled leaf amongst debris.

Scientific name *Arachnura scorpionoides.*
Female Size $2/3$in.
Male Size $1/12$in.
Habitat Forests, gardens, shrubby areas, reeds and swamps.
Range Africa and Madagascar.

$2/3$in

TREE STUMP ORB-WEAVER

A nocturnal spider which dismantles its web daily and rebuilds it each evening. During the day, the female sits tightly, resembling part of a tree branch. Her abdomen has many protuberances which help camouflage her. The male is very dark and hunched.

Scientific name *Poltys illepidus*.
Female Size $3/8$in.
Male Size $1/6$in.
Habitat Forest edges, grassland, gardens.
Range Asia, India, Japan, Australia.

$3/8$in

ORNATE ORB-WEAVER

This spider has a pearly, spotted abdomen which is flat. The carapace is gray and orange. The web is difficult to spot as it lies parallel to the bark of a tree. The female sits on a lace-like area near the hub of the web. The male is small with no ornate abdomen.

Scientific name *Herennia ornatissima*.
Female Size $1/2$in.
Male Size $1/6$in.
Habitat Tree trunks, rock faces in forested areas.
Range SE Asia.

$1/2$in

HORNED ORB-WEAVER

This is a spiny-backed spider. The female has a hard, wide abdomen with sharp, curved spines. The web can be built in between trees in either full sunlight or shade, at dawn and removed at dusk.

Scientific name *Gasteracantha falcicornis.*
Female Size $1/3$in.
Male Size $1/12$in.
Habitat Tropical rainforest and gardens.
Range Africa.

THORN SPIDER

A black, shiny spider whose yellow abdomen has a pair of large spines. In the daytime, the spider hangs upside down from the hub of the web. They have few enemies except solitary wasps. The male resembles an ant.

Scientific name *Microthena schreibersi.*
Female Size $3/8$in.
Male Size $1/8$in.
Habitat Forests and shady places.
Range Central America.

SPOTTED WOLF SPIDER

This is a small spider with a mottled appearance, thin legs and colored brown. There is a pale central band on the carapace and chevrons on the abdomen. When the spiderlings hatch, the mother carries the young on her back.

Scientific name *Pardosa amentata*.
Female Size $1/3$in.
Male Size $1/6$in.
Habitat Grassland, fields, lawns and roadsides.
Range Europe much of Asia.

$1/3$in

WOLF WEAVER

One of the few wolf spiders which spins a web. They have purplish-brown legs and body with narrow pale bands. The female has two flexible spinnerets on the abdomen where she attaches the egg sac. They construct a funnel where the spiders hide beside the web, when waiting for prey.

Scientific name *Hippasa foveifera.*
Female Size $3/8$in.
Male Size $1/3$in.
Habitat Lawns, grassland, forest clearings.
Range Africa.

$3/8$in

PIRATE SPIDER

This is a semi-aquatic spider, spending much of its time under water. The carapace is green-brown and marked with a 'V' design. The abdomen has purple and white spots and is velvety. The web consists of a vertical tube made in moss which can be closed by drawing across a silk veil. The bottom is open to water.

Scientific name *Pirata piraticus.*
Female Size $^1/_3$in.
Male Size $^1/_6$in.
Habitat Marshes, pond and lake edges.
Range Europe, Asia, N America, Japan.

$^1/_3$in

NURSERY WEB SPIDER

The female spider requires a present from the male of an insect wrapped in silk before she will mate. Both sexes are gray-brown with a pale stripe on the carapace. The legs are long. The huge egg sac is carried underneath the female's abdomen.

Scientific name *Pisaura mirabilis.*
Female Size $^1/_2$in.
Male Size $^3/_8$in.
Habitat Woods, meadows, heaths, gardens and scrub.
Range Europe, Asia, N Africa.

$^1/_2$in

FISHING SPIDER

This spider is dark brown with two cream or white bands running the length of the body. It can sometimes be known by the names Swamp or Raft Spider. The spider hunts by spreading its legs on the water surface to feel the presence of insects. It also vibrates its legs to attract prey and is able to haul a small fish ashore.

Scientific name *Dolomedes fimbriatus.*
Female Size $5/6$in.
Male Size $1/2$in.
Habitat Lakes, ponds, swamps, streams.
Range Europe, Asia.

5/16in

AMERICAN GREEN LYNX SPIDER

An athletic, green spider with red and black markings in the male. The legs are spiny and long, with a tapering abdomen. The spider runs across vegetation and through the undergrowth with great speed and agility.

Scientific name *Peucetia viridans*.
Female Size 2/3in.
Male Size 3/8in.
Habitat Grassland and shrubby places.
Range Southern USA, Central America.

AFRICAN GREEN LYNX SPIDER

A green spider with very long yellow-green legs and dark bands. They leap through leaves to chase prey or escape from predators. The leg span can reach 1$\frac{1}{2}$in and they are believed to be able to jump $\frac{3}{4}$in to catch flying insects.

Scientific name *Peucetia sp.*
Female Size $\frac{1}{2}$in.
Male Size Unknown.
Habitat Savannah, shrubs and grasses.
Range S Africa.

$\frac{1}{2}$in

MOUSE SPIDER

This spider seems mouse-like with its gray, furry abdomen. In Europe, the spider is nocturnal, wandering on walls where it looks for insects. They do build a web but most of its time is spent hunting. They occasionally bite.

Scientific name *Micaria pulicaria.*
Female Size $3/8$in.
Male Size $1/3$in.
Habitat Buildings, holes in walls, under tree bark.
Range Europe, N America, Asia.

RUSTY WANDERING SPIDER

A rust-colored and fast moving spider whose entire body is orange-brown, including the legs. A darker brown band runs across the carapace and the abdomen. They hunt by lying in ambush and attacking, at great speed, any prey that comes close.

Scientific name *Cupiennius getazi.*
Female Size $1^1/_4$in.
Male Size $^7/_8$in.
Habitat Tropical rainforest.
Range Central America.

$1^1/_4$in

MALAYSIAN HUNTSMAN

A long-legged spider which is active at night. Olive-brown in color but paler on top with a dark band down the middle of the carapace. There is a thick covering of hairs over the body and legs. The nest is made out of two leaves stuck together with silk.

Scientific name *Isopeda sp.*
Female Size 1¹/4in.
Male Size ⁷/8in.
Habitat Tropical rainforest.
Range Malaysia.

1¹/4in

LICHEN HUNTSMAN

Cleverly camouflaged against mossy tree trunks, this spider is very difficult to see. It moves at great speed when disturbed. The hairs on the legs help to blur the outline of the spiders and reduces shadows. Both sexes are similar in appearance.

Scientific name *Pandercetes gracilis.*
Female Size ²/3in.
Male Size ¹/2in.
Habitat Tropical forests.
Range Australia, New Guinea.

2/3in

FOREST HUNTSMAN

Well camouflaged against tree trunks, this spider has hairy legs which reduce shadows and blur the outline as it lies close to the trunk waiting for prey. The eight eyes are grouped together on the carapace.

Scientific name *Pandercetes plumipes*.
Female Size $2/3$in.
Male Size $3/8$in.
Habitat Grassland and shrubby places, in sandy or chalky areas.
Range Europe, N Africa, W Asia.

$2/3$in

HEATHER SPIDER

The colors of this spider can be one of pink, yellow or white depending on the color of the flower on which it is found. They ambush their prey. The carapace of the female has two horn-like projections near the eyes. The male is smaller, orange-brown with dark legs.

Scientific name *Thomisus onustus.*
Female Size 1/3in.
Male Size 1/6in.
Habitat Heathers in heathland, meadows.
Range Europe, N Africa, Asia, Japan.

WHITE CRAB SPIDER

The carapace and legs of this spider are translucent white, the abdomen is pure white with a black spot at each corner. The color can be yellow or pink. The male is brown and appears to be unrelated as it is so different.

Scientific name *Thomisus spectabilis.*
Female Size 3/8in.
Male Size 1/12in.
Habitat Tropical forests and gardens.
Range SE Asia.

COMMON CRAB SPIDER

This species ambushes its prey, grabbing them with its front legs. The carapace of the female has a pale band with a triangular mark. The abdomen is marked with chevrons. The male is small and dark and, during courtship, wraps the female loosely in silk.

Scientific name *Xysticus* cristatus.
Female Size $1/3$in.
Male Size $1/6$in.
Habitat Undergrowth in woodlands and grasslands.
Range Europe, N Africa, Asia.

$1/3$in

FLOWER SPIDER

The color of this spider blends in to the color of the flower it is visiting, waiting to ambush prey. The female can be white, yellow or green, slowly changing between colors. The abdomen can be striped red. The male has a brown carapace and legs with a buff-colored abdomen. The female readily attacks insects much larger than herself and is a formidable predator.

Scientific name *Misumena vatia*.
Female Size $1/3$in.
Male Size $1/6$in.
Habitat Flowery meadows and gardens.
Range Europe, N Africa, Asia, Japan, N America.

$1/3$in

BIRD DROPPING SPIDER

At rest, this spider resembles a bird dropping. The surface has a wet and lumpy look due to the blobs and warts over the black and white surface. It lies very still with its legs drawn in waiting for prey, for hours at a time. It also can emit a smell to attract flies which it grabs with its legs.

Scientific name *Phrynarachne rugosa.*
Female Size $1/3$in.
Male Size $1/6$in.
Habitat Tropical forests.
Range Africa, Madagascar.

GRASS JUMPER

This spider has a shiny carapace and dark, velvety-brown abdomen. The eyes are in three rows. The male has a white face and the first pair of legs have tufts of white hairs. The nests are made in dead grasses and plants.

Scientific name *Evarcha flammata*.
Female Size $1/4$in.
Male Size $1/6$in.
Habitat Grassland and heathland.
Range Europe, N America, Asia.

$1/4$in

FENCE-POST JUMPER

This spider has a very flat body so that it can rest beneath peeling bark or under stones. The carapace of the female is dark brown and the abdomen is gray-brown with chevron patterning. The male is darker than the female. They often hunt in the late afternoon.

Scientific name *Marpissa mucosa.*
Female Size $1/3$in.
Male Size $1/3$in.
Habitat Woodland edges, trees, hedges, fence posts, stone walls.
Range Europe, Asia.

$1/3$in

PANTROPICAL JUMPER

Like most jumping spiders, the carapace is rectangular and in the male, is as large as the abdomen. These are common spiders in warm countries. The female has pale marks on her abdomen and a pale patch in the middle of the carapace. The male is more marked, than the female, and has either a white central band or spots along the body.

Scientific name *Plexippus paykulli.*
Female Size $3/8$in.
Male Size $1/3$in.
Habitat Woodlands, plantations, rocks, buildings, gardens.
Range Tropical and subtropical regions such as Japan and Southern USA.

BEAUTIFUL JUMPER

This spider has a bold appearance. The female carapace is black and the abdomen and front legs are orange-red. The male carapace is black and the red abdomen has a black band. The legs of the male are white at the back and orange at the front. The bright colors are used in courtship as the two sexes dance and weave their legs.

Scientific name *Philaeus chrysops.*
Female Size $3/8$in.
Male Size $1/3$in.
Habitat Woodland, heathland, scrub and rocks.
Range Europe, Africa, Asia.

$3/8$in

BLACK SPOTTED JUMPER

The markings on this spider are bold and give a warning to others to keep away. The orange and black is intended to mimic a distasteful insect which predators would avoid.

Scientific name *Acragus sp.*
Female Size $1/3$in.
Male Size $1/3$in.
Habitat Tropical rainforest.
Range Argentina, Brazil.

ZEBRA JUMPER

This spider stalks its prey on walls and does not fall off. It launches itself with the four back legs only after fixing a safety line to the ground. They have very good vision to identify prey. The carapace is shiny black and the abdomen is brown or black with three white bands. The jaws of the male are huge, and are used to restrain the female during mating.

Scientific name *Salticus scenicus*.
Female Size $1/4$in.
Male Size $1/6$in.
Habitat Walls, trees, buildings, rocks.
Range Europe, N America, Asia.

$1/4$in

EUROPEAN HARVESTMAN

The name comes from the fact that they are numerous at harvest-time. They have no silk or venom glands. Their very long legs are used to find small insects. The body is gray-brown, in one piece, and two eyes sit back to back on the tubercle. The female is larger than the male.

Scientific name *Leiobunum rotundum.*
Female Size ¹/₄in.
Male Size ¹/₈in.
Habitat Woods, fields, hedges.
Range Europe.

RED SPIDER MITE

These are minute relatives of spiders. They often appear in huge numbers and are known for their ability to produce silk from their mouthparts. They are serious pest, feeding on plants and crops. Often, they invade homes in the summer. They can be orange or red.

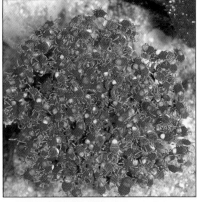

Scientific name *Tetranychus sp.*
Female Size ¹/₃₂in.
Male Size ¹/₃₂in.
Habitat Agricultural land, gardens, heathland, woods.
Range Worldwide.

AFRICAN CAMEL SPIDER

Also known a sun spiders, wind scorpions and solifugids. These are fast running creatures with huge, forward-projecting jaws. Most hunt prey at night. The legs are slender and long, with many erect hairs. When running, they can appear to be a ball of fluff.

Scientific name *Solpuga sp.*
Female Size 1^1/2in.
Male Size 1^1/4in.
Habitat Dry, sandy arid areas.
Range S Africa.

AFRICAN WHIP SCORPION

These spiders are bizarre-looking but harmless. They have no tail. They use long, spiny pedipalps to grab insects. The first pair of legs are very long and whip-like. They are not used for walking but to sense prey from a distance. The appearance is mottled with legs that are banded light and dark.

Scientific name *Damon variegatus.*
Female Size 1^1/3in.
Male Size 1^1/4in.
Habitat Caves, mines, empty homes.
Range E Africa.

RELATED SPECIES

Index

INDEX